SIDNEY DEAN

James Fenimore Cooper's Leatherstocking

Symbol of the American Nation

Copyright © 2024 by Sidney Dean

All rights reserved. No part of this publication may be reproduced, stored or transmitted in any form or by any means, electronic, mechanical, photocopying, recording, scanning, or otherwise without written permission from the publisher. It is illegal to copy this book, post it to a website, or distribute it by any other means without permission.

First edition

This book was professionally typeset on Reedsy. Find out more at reedsy.com

Contents

Introduction	1
Chapter 1	3
Chapter 2	11
Chapter 3	19
Chapter 4	44
Chapter 5	52

Introduction

Cooper's Leatherstocking is the first unmistakably American archetype representative of the United States, an incarnation of the American Spirit. The five books comprising the *Leatherstocking Tales* cover the gamut of the American frontier experience from colonial times to the beginnings of the "winning of the West." Through the central character, wilderness scout Natty Bumppo, Cooper presents the major currents of American attitude toward nature, civilization, and expansion, and depicts the complicated white-Indian relationship. Cooper is the first author to present all vital domestic factors which participated in forming the American national character through the first quarter of the nineteenth century.

Natty Bumppo serves his purpose of incorporating the American nation, people, and spirit in two ways. In the guise of a common man living and acting on the dynamic edge of the frontier, he guides the reader through the formative eras of development of the distinctly American identity. On the metaphysical level, he represents the American Spirit, with its blend of European and New World traditions and ways, its independent mind and quest for personal liberty. In this latter function he also serves as mentor for upcoming generations of leaders who will have to provide America with a viable order, but who in the process will be called upon to retain the values for which generations of immigrants worked and for which the War of Independence and the War of 1812 were fought.

Cooper created this American archetype to fuse together the American people who, in the aftermath of the War of 1812 were just beginning to develop a deeper sense of national identity and cultural autonomy; by showing the depth of American history, he hoped to instill a firm feeling of belonging, especially among non-elites. Additionally, he hoped to influence political developments to preserve the spirit of individual liberty for which the Revolution had been fought. Finally, Leatherstocking serves as a forum to warn against throwing away the nation's resources for populist political purposes, and advocates a policy of respect for and conciliation with Native Americans.

Chapter 1

AMERICAN LITERATURE BEFORE COOPER

Slow Development of American Cultural Identity

Even after the Revolution, Americans remained intellectually closer to the Mother Country than to one-another. The thirteen states of the original Union, diverse economically, culturally, and ethnically, needed a common bond to cement the young nation. Foreign and defense policy could be cited as practical reasons for cooperation, but lent little support to popular acceptance of identification. The task of forging a unified cultural tradition for the new nation remained to be accomplished – it was up to the birth of a distinct American literature to secure this aim.

Early United States Novelists

The few quality writers of fiction in the early United States remained largely European in their approach, and failed to "set ablaze the hearts and minds of the American masses," as Wilbur Zelinsky graphically formulates.[1] The most impressive "American" writing in the late eighteenth/early nineteenth centuries was still "non-fiction,"[2] mostly of religious or political nature. The "historical novels" written before Cooper were more properly historical narratives, dramatized accounts of real events, not novels in the contemporary sense of the word.[3] No early novelist before Cooper was able to match a Thomas Jefferson or a Tom Paine with regard to passion or pace.[4]

To briefly mention the most distinguished U.S. writers of "literature" before Cooper:

*Charles Brockden Brown, the only popular American writer to precede Cooper with an historical romance along the general lines of the Leatherstocking character (*Arthur Mervyn*, 1799) remained much more continental in his conventions than Cooper would, and failed to capture the same reception afforded Cooper. Much of his work was strongly marked by Gothic horror elements popular in England and continental Europe at the time. Financially, he was not able to sustain himself through his fiction writing, working primarily as a journalist.[5] Also, Brown did not create the deepseated philosophical and nationalist symbolism which Cooper systematically provided with the Leatherstocking cycle;

*Hugh Henry Breckenridge's 1792 novel *Modern Chivalry* contained Frontier settings and some fully American elements, but it remained a political burlesque in the European manner;[6]

*William Cullen Bryant, Cooper's contemporary was a poet and essayist/critic, not a novelist/romancier, placing him outside competition with Cooper for the honor of the first truly American writer of fiction;

*Washington Irving, often considered the leading "American" writer contemporary with Cooper, crafted his stories mostly along European models, frequently invoking the tool of satire – itself a primarily "European" approach, even if some American political writers of the Revolutionary and post-revolutionary era employed it for partisan purposes. Irving himself saw his primary contribution to American culture in his multi-volume histories and biographies rather than in his fiction.[7] Washington Irving, together with William Cullen Bryant and William Gilmore Simms the most prestigious and successful of Cooper's contemporary American authors, did not turn to the Frontier as a topic until ten years after Cooper, and then pursued this most fundamental of American themes as novelistically written history/biography rather than as straight fiction.

Popular and Critical Orientation Toward Europe

American authors who felt they had economic or artistic potential frequently did not bother seeking publication in the United States, but sent their manuscripts directly to British or Continental publishers – of course, these authors stayed with accepted European conventions in order to ensure their success.[8] But even those American authors who wrote for the domestic audience tended to emulate British and Continental European style. American publishers regularly waited to see how a book sold overseas before investing in a US edition, further driving American writers to satisfy foreign tastes before domestic. Of no small significance was the continued orientation of some American critics toward the English model. Grossman cites how American reviewers awaited the praise of British critics for Cooper's early works before daring to laud him themselves.[9]

No American fiction writer before Cooper was able to sustain himself financially with this work. Lack of effective copyright protection added to the dilemma of America authors, as booksellers in the New World could simply reprint British or European "bestsellers" without paying the royalties due local writers.[10] Charles Jared Ingersoll provides some relevant statistics for the early 1820s: Approximately 2-3 Million Dollars worth of books were sold annually (two Dollars was considered a steep price, indicating sales of approximately one million books yearly among a population of 9.6 million [1820 census]); 135 copyrights were issued to Americans during the January 1822 - April 1823 timeframe, but Ingersoll stresses that most American writers secured no copyright.[11] Of course, the book sales figures include considerable numbers of imports.

This coincided with a continued preference of American readers for European motifs and settings. The American reading public still labored under the misconception that the prosaic, mercantilist United States lacked the romantic elements to inspire a novelist. An American work of fiction, lacking lords and ladies, castles and keeps, swords and sorcerers, simply could not be good. So why bother to read one?[12] Even nationalist literat Walter Channing considered America's "want [of] a remote antiquity" to equate "want of a vast variety of topicks, of the very first interest in literature."[13] For that matter, Cooper apologized in the preface of his first "American" novel, *The Spy*, for the setting lacking such interesting aspects as castles and lords, or, in James Grossman's words, "any of the other artificial distinctions of life which made English novels so attractive to American readers..."[14]

This defensive cultural posture was enforced by prevalent arguments such as:

*primacy of linguistic and cultural ties to England;

*the thesis that America's "wilderness" automatically precluded erudition and culture capable of reaching European levels;

* "the much debated thesis advanced by [French scientist Georges Leclerc] Buffon...that the human race inevitably deteriorates in the Western hemisphere."[15]

The Challenge to Create a National Literature

American intellectual elites were aware of the cultural vacuum, and determined to create a national literature, a literary declaration of independence.[16] They aspired to a "national" literature for two equally vital reasons: to demonstrate (to Americans and Europeans alike) that America need not take a back place behind Europe in the cultural arena, and to foster national cohesion and identity during the early and precarious years of independence.[17]

The *North American Review* was founded in 1815 as a weapon in the war for cultural autonomy. For the first five years of its existence, the founders debated in its bimonthly pages the issues surrounding the search for an American literature.

Walter Channing fired the opening shots with his "Essay on American Language and Literature" and "Reflections on the Literary Delinquency of America," in the September and November 1815 issues, respectively.[18] His "Essay" proposed that the "melancholy record" of American letters would be reversed once Americans awakened to appreciate the unique and distinctive nature of life in the New World. He stressed that literature germinates from native peculiarities of its country of origin, including climate, institutions, and relations (i.e. political, religious, moral), and advocated development of a distinctly American language, i.e. linguistic peculiarities setting the United States off from Britain, to foster development of a distinctly American literature. In 1821, J.G. Palfrey called for American novelists to use the country's early history as source material.[19]

The condescending to overbearing attitude of European, especially British critics, toward American literature peaked in Sidney Smith's 1820 quip: "In the four quarters of the globe, who reads am American book?" (Evidently the occasional American to read such literature was a nonentity to Smith's mind). Among the American elites to pick up Smith's gauntlet was James Fenimore Cooper, who credibly claimed to have written his first work, the novel of manners Precaution (1820), simply to show that anyone could write a book in the British style.[20] Precaution sold well in England, despite its mediocre quality. Cooper in 1821 wrote a truly American novel, *The Spy* (set in the War of Independence), followed by *The Pioneers* (1823). Smith soon had his answer, as American and European readers flocked to Cooper.

[1] Zelinsky, Wilbur. Nation Into State. Chapel Hill, 1988, p. 166.

CHAPTER 1

[2] Meserole, H.T. American Literature: Tradition and Innovation. Lexington (MA) 1969. P. 340.

[3] Leisy, E.E. The American Historical Novel. Norman (OK) 1950. P. 9.

[4] Walter Channing, himself a champion of American efforts to achieve literary respect, found that few early writers of the republic could pass the test of domestic, let alone foreign critics; he went so far as to term the few truly great writers of non-fiction, e.g. Benjamin Franklin, as men whose achievements belong to mankind rather than marking a national institution. See his "Reflections on the Literary Delinquency of America," North American Review, Nov. 1815, reprinted in Spiller, Revolution, pp. 112-131.

[5] See R. Lewis, The American Adam, Chicago 1955, pp. 92 ff. for discussion of Brown's place in early American literature, and the European aspects of his work; A. Taylor, William Cooper's Town, NY, 1995, p. 407, on Brown's lack of commercial success.

[6] Meserole, pp. 609-610.

[7] For discussion of Irving's place in American literature and his primarily European conventions, see, for example, W.E. Channing, "Remarks on National Literature," in The Christian Examiner, XXXVI, January 1830, pp. 269-94.

[8] Robert Spiller, The American Literary Revolution, 1783-1837,, NY, 1967, passim.

[9] James Grossman, James Fenimore Cooper, NY 1949, pp. 28-29.

[10] See for example, Grossman, . 64; Spiller, Revolution, p. viii and pp. 392-98.

[11] C.J. Ingersoll, "Discourse Concerning the Influence of America on the Mind," delivered 1823 to the American Philological Society; reprinted in Spiller, Revolution, pp. 239 ff.

[12] Spiller, *Revolution*, Preface; Taylor, *Town*, p. 407.

[13] Channing, "Reflections.

[14] Grossman, p. 24.

[15] Spiller, Revolution, p. 4. Also see Grossman, p. 67, on even benevolent European commentators looking down upon American breeding and education, showering Cooper with patronizing friendliness during his European stay (1826-32).

[16] Zelinsky, p. 166.

[17] [1]. Zelinsky cites seven sources which have "documented in detail" this effort: R.W. Bollwell, "Concerning the Study of Nationalism in American Literature," American Literature 10:405-16; E. A. Bradsher, "The Rise of Nationalism in American Literature," in. N. Caffee & T.A. Kirby (eds.) Studies for William Alexander Read, (Baton Rouge: LSU Press, 1940); R. Ketcham, From Colony to Country: The Revolution in American Thought, 1750-1820 (New York, Macmillan, 1974); R.B. Nye, The Cultural Life of the New Nation, 1776-1830 (London: Hamish Hamilton, 1960); K. Silverman, A Cultural History of the American Revolution...1776-1789 (New York, Crowell, 1971); B.T. Spencer, "A National Literature, 1837-1855," American Literature 8:125-59; D.L. Werner, The Idea of Union in American Verse, 1776-1876 (Ph.D. Diss., U. Penn., 1932); also see Spiller, Revolution, passim.

[18] Reprinted in Spiller, Revolution, pp. 112-131.

[19] Leisy, p. 43.

[20] The primary source for Cooper's decision to take up writing is his daughter Alice, who relates his disgust over his wife's reading of second-rate British novels. This is related in detail in Taylor, Town, Ch. 15, and in other sources.

Chapter 2

ARCHETYPE AND NATIONAL MYTH

Culture and National Identity

The various definitions scholars provide for the concept "national identity" or equivalent terms agree on the core elements of: self-identification at the national level overriding all lower-level group identifications, be the regional, clan, professional, religious, or class; common heritage and culture as a significant bond; acknowledgement of or desire for common statehood and co-habitation in one nation-state. In Hans Kohn's words, "nationalism is, first and foremost, a state of mind..." The role of culture, including literature, in defining national identity through provision of symbols and myth, is well established.[1]

Historians and anthropologists generally agree on the nature of national myth as the fruit of processing historical experience into literary narrative filled with evocative symbolism. This national myth is vital to the self-identification of the nation-group (regardless of whether or not this group forms a nation-state), and to its vision of its own place in the world. History and the expressed ideals or ideology of the group become abstracted to take the form of what Slotkin calls "icons" which evoke specific powerful reactions, more on the emotional or instinctive than the intellectual level.[2] The essential myths of a society will center around those issues which concern that society most deeply and most persistently.

There is no dispute over the vital role writers have played in fostering national identity among many peoples; movements such as *Giovanni Italia*, *Junges Deutschland*, Young Poland, and the various Slavophile movements in the nineteenth century, and individual writers such as Allesandro Manzoni, Friedrich Schiller, Henryk Sienkiewicz, and Robert Burns are but a few examples of the dynamic effect of the literati on mass politics in Europe. One of the primary tools of patriotic literature has been the historical romance, which symbiotically encouraged the development of nationalist sentiment in many nations in the 19th century, and was in turn welcomed because it appealed to nascent nationalist/patriotic instincts. The genre works by grasping the formative events which crystalize the emergence of the nation or people, and recounting them in a heroic depiction rife with symbolism, apt to mythologize the described events. Simultaneously a connection is drawn to modern issues and conflicts, suggesting an unbroken and relevant connection between the fog-shrouded past and the present.[3] In the words of William Gilmore Simms, who began writing just a few years after Cooper, and who attained almost the same popularity during his lifetime:

The modern Romance is the substitute which the people of the present day offer for the ancient epic. The form is changed; the matter is very much the same; at all events, it differs much more seriously from the English novel than it does from the epic and the drama, because the difference is one of material, even more than of fabrication.[4]

Or as E.E. Leisy succinctly concluded, "the historical novel satisfies a desire for national homogeneity."[5]

The American Frontier Myth

The "American Myth" is largely the "Myth of the Frontier." The roots of this go back to colonial times, but it did not flourish until the early-to-mid nineteenth century, as ever larger portions of the American population lived east of the frontier. Slotkin concludes:

The Myth of the Frontier was developed by and for an America that was a colonial offshoot of Europe, agrarian in economy, localist in politics, tentative as to nationality, and relatively homogenous in ethnicity, language, and religion... [6]

The reason for this development seems clear. As a greater percentage of the population lived in "civilized" regions of the country (despite the continued expansion of the frontier), the dangers and sacrifices of the preceding Pioneer generations took on mythic proportions, affording a medium of common identification for citizens who came from diverse backgrounds to a new land.[7] The Frontier Myth became a metaphor for America's existence and justification. The negative image most emigrants brought of Europe became transferred and associated with the most European aspects of America: the cities and the semi-feudal system of landlords-over-sharecroppers. The move westward, to the wild frontier, paralleled emigration from decadent and stifling Europe to the wild New World. Ascribing inherent superiority to the frontier, despite (or perhaps because of) the regression to more primitive lifestyle when compared with towns and villages, was the natural development of the renunciation of the established order of Europe. In effect, the pioneers who picked up and moved west searching for a better, freer life, repeated the thirteen colonies' declaration of independence on a microcosmic scale; this was especially the case with the woodsmen who rejected societal constraints completely, preferring to live according to "natural" laws and adapt to native ways when this seemed the reasonable thing to do. Slotkin defines this process of evolution:

The completed American was therefore one who remade his fortune and his character by an emigration, a setting forth for newer and richer lands,; by isolation and regression to a more primitive manner of life; and by establishing his political position in opposition to both the Indian and European, the New World savage and the Old World aristocracy.[8]

If this denial of central authority meant forfeiture of the benefits available from belonging to that society, so be it – personal salvation and integrity was more important to Leatherstocking, and to the nation of people he represented, than creature comforts. The continued mobility westward, away from the arm of authority, which Natty embodies is the metaphor of the American drive for personal, political, and cultural independence – the core of the American national mentality and its reason for being.

Historian Frederick Jackson Turner, who created the seminal

1893 essay about the Frontier, concluded that the Frontier is what made America distinct from all other nations: "American social development has been continually beginning over again on the frontier. This perennial rebirth, this fluidity of American life, this expansion westward with its new opportunities, its continuing touch with the simplicity of primitive society, furnished the forces dominating American character."[9] The distinct American identity arose with the creation and veneration of the Frontier Hero - "a new breed of idol for whom there is no clear precedent in the Old World or Colonial America."[10] Real-life heroes of this ilk include first and foremost Daniel Boone and Davy Crockett, but also their first and foremost literary progeny, Natty Bumppo.

In this function Bumppo, like Crockett in real life, was best suited to express the yearnings of Americans "seeking a middle ground in a civilization that still kept contact with nature."[11] Early "non-fiction"[12] books on the lives of frontier heroes such as Daniel Boone (especially John Filson's *Kentucke*, published in 1784) preceded or coincided with Cooper's novels, and helped beget interest in the Frontier as a truly American literary subject.[13]

Cooper proceeded to popularize the Frontier as a setting for American national literature, simultaneously entertaining and steeped in symbolism and meaning. The protagonist of the Frontier novel is recognized by readers as a mythic hero with symbolic relevance, who "had gone to conquer a mythic region whose hidden magic was to be tapped only by self-reliant individualists, capable of enduring the lonesome reach."[14]

A core thesis of the Myth of the Frontier is the concept of national expansion marked by an epic-scale struggle between Indian and white, as well as by conflict between different social and regional interests within the white community. The rapid expansion westward inherently bore the race, or rather land, struggle with it. While British policy had preserved a fairly stable border between Indian territory and colonial territory (many of the eighteenth-century "Indian Wars" were actually proxy wars pitting tribes allied with France against the British settlers, and vice-versa), the Ordinance of 1787 which opened the Trans-Allegheny frontier to American settlers immediately dispossessed the great Iroquois nation, among other tribes – a feature to be repeated over and over until the final subjugation of tenable Indian resistance in the 1880s. Had a slower, stable rate of migration been agreed upon, an accommodation might have been found, allowing for assimilation or neighborly relations between the two peoples – or so the vision of many white Americans even in the early nineteenth century, many of whom did not conceal their bad consciences regarding land-capture and genocide. A vital factor in the deep popular commitment to the Myth of the Frontier is this vision it proffered of resolving these disharmonies. On the one hand, the natural and aboriginal dangers presented by the frontier worked to overcome the differences between North and South, farmer and hunter, sharecropper and landlord. On the other hand, there remained the ideal, expressed in the Leatherstocking character, of ultimately achieving harmony between the races, with each group learning from the other, to create a superior society. While there was early "Indian fighter" literature, and the Leatherstocking cycle contains plentiful conflict with "bad" Indians, the stereotype portrayal of racial and cultural incompatibility arose with American expansion into the Great Plains toward the middle of the nineteenth century.[15]

CHAPTER 2

[1] Kohn (The Idea of Nationalism [New York, 1944]) cited in David Potter, History and American Society, NY 1973, p. 63. Also see Leisy, Ch. 1; Lewis, Ch. 1; Potter, pp. 51-56, 63-77; Slotkin, passim; Zelinsky, pp. 4 ff., pp. 13 ff. for a discussion of various definitions of national identity and for importance of symbolism and myth to national identity.

[2] For detailed discussions of this nature and function of national myth, see Leisy, Ch. 1; Slotkin (esp. Ch. 1).

[3] For discussion on the connection between historical romance and development of national identity, see Leisy, passim; Potter, pp. 69-84; Sheppard, passim; Slotkin, passim. Slotkin also provides a sizeable bibliography on the genre of historical romance and its political impact.

[4] From the preface to The Yemassee (1835), quoted in Folsom, pp. 19-20.

[5] Leisy, p. 4.

[6] Slotkin, p. 15. For discussion of the "American Myth" see also Lewis, Ch. 1

[7] See Slotkin, passim, for in-depth analysis of the Frontier Myth; also Folsom, passim, for the Frontier Myth as presented through "Western" literature; Potter, 120 ff. on the appeal of the Frontier Myth to the immigrant nation.

[8] Slotkin, p. 35. See also Barker, p. 11, on the American Dream and the Frontier Myth; Lawrence, p. 13; O'Connor, on early America's search for innocence as part of the American Dream, and the inherent burden of "the need to be a perfect society, or as near to perfect as possible." pp. iii-iv; Leisy, pp. 50 ff., and Taylor, Town, passim, for the landlord-tenant conflict; W. Motley, The American Abraham, NY 1987, p. 16, on the Frontier as the symbol of Revolution.

[9] Turner, "The Significance of the Frontier in American

History," 1893; cited in Barker, p. 11; see also Folsom, p. 17; Potter, pp. 110-111.

[10] Zelinsky, P. 43. See also House, p. 73, and Perkins, pp. 490-92 on the Leatherstocking Tales as the first materialization of the Frontier hero in literature; Potter, 230 ff., 331, on the appeal of the Frontier Hero to the American people.

[11] ibid.

[12] Actually these "biographical" accounts were highly sensationalized, both for dramatic effect and to further the reputations of the individuals, who frequently had economic or political agendas. At best they might satisfy the definition of today's dramatized renditions of actual events, sometimes termed "faction."

[13] [1]. Factual and fictional accounts of early explorations, in the Americas and elsewhere, do not fit this operating definition, as the vital element of "Frontier" is missing: the shifting border between wilderness and civilization, the goal of expanding settlements of the new land. Likewise, "Borderer" fiction of Britain or Central Europe does not take place in the same type of unknown setting as American Frontier literature.

[14] Slotkin, p. 11.

[15] See Folsom, passim; Motley, pp. 22-23; Slotkin, passim.

Chapter 3

NATTY BUMPPO AS THE AMERICAN ARCHETYPE

Leatherstocking and the American Spirit

Cooper uses the vehicle of the romance to create the larger-than-life character of Natty Bumppo, who acts as embodiment of the American spirit and as narrator for the passage of events shaping the nation's development. Like other great American writers, Cooper realized the romance was the suitable vehicle for conveying epic, mythological concepts.[1] His central character serves as incarnation of the essential themes. Cooper himself spoke of his intent to "study American character" which was to be the essence of his novels. His fictional characters were intended to "relate past, present, and possible Americans to one another."[2]

On the surface, Leatherstocking represents the colonial America which has lived in a new environment and developed away from its European roots. He was raised by the Delaware Indian nation, and trained to survive and excel in their environment. The gap between the Frontiersman and the Easterners, even if they come from cities less than a hundred miles from the "Wilderness," is obvious in Leatherstocking's disdain for "wasty" ways and the Easterners' lack of insight into the "new world" they enter. The sacrifice of British lives in *Mohicans* and *Pathfinder* because arrogance and ignorance prevent the soldiers from adjusting their style of combat is one case in point. *Mohicans*' Major Heyward epitomizes this failure to understand and adjust to the new environment, projecting the playing fields of Eaton into the Wilderness:

It is possible that the Indians and stragglers of the enemy may intrude [on the withdrawing British women], in which case you will remind them of the terms of the capitulation, and threaten to report their conduct to Montcalm. A word will suffice.[204]

Leatherstocking and the Indian

Leatherstocking's relationship with the Native Americans is a central theme of the *Tales*, and one of the most significant with regard to the stories' national symbolism.

Cooper clearly depicts people, regardless of their race or nationality, as being faulty. Some have flawed characters, others are foolish; some are rapacious, others well-meaning, but left to their own devices, people hurt one-another and damage the God-given order. Natty Bumppo's frequent allusion to "red" and "white" gifts, and his explaining the virtues of Indian ways to whites and vice versa, clearly shows he considers neither group inherently superior to the other in terms of morals or wisdom. "God made all three [races] alike," Deerslayer argues against his friend Harry's racist theories:

He made us, in the main, much the same in feelin's, though I'll not deny that he gave each race its gifts. A white man's gifts are Christianized, while a redskin's are more for the wilderness. Thus, it would be a great offense for a white man to scalp the dead, wheras it's a signal vartue in an Indian. Then ag'in, a white man cannot amboosh women and children in war, while a redskin may. 'Tis cruel work, I'll allow, but for them its lawful work, while for us it would be grievous work...but I will maintain that tradition, and use, and color, and laws make such a difference in races as to amount to gifts. I do not deny that there are tribes among the Indians that are nat'rally pervarse and wicked, as there are nations among the whites [e.g. Mingos and French]...[41]

Natty's frequent allusion to "gifts" presents the differences inherent in the two cultures, as well as the potential and the limitations for synthesis.

Leatherstocking's views are frequently ambivalent, as befits one torn between two identities, not quite fitting into either. He criticizes white treatment of the Indian and the hypocrisy of Christian missionary zeal. His reply to Minister Grant concerning Chingachgook's approach to death in *Pioneers* clearly faults "civilization" for changing the land into an environment in which the Indian neither can, nor wishes to, survive:

He is old and stiff, and you have made the game so scarce and shy, that better shots than him find it hard to get a livelihood. Now he thinks he shall travel where it will always be good hunting; where no wicked or unjust Indians can go; and where he shall meet all his tribe together ag'in.[400-401]

In *Deerslayer* he proposes that Heaven is multi-racial, and that the righteous of all nations and peoples will meet there.[422-425]

On the other hand, Natty Bumppo is also very much the "Indian fighter" of later Western fiction. Analog to the political alignments of the colonial and post-colonial era, in which certain polities allied with certain Indian tribes, to make joint venture against both the white's and the Indian tribe's traditional enemies, Leatherstocking is friend of the Delaware (and later, in *Prairie*, the Pawnee), but deadly opponent of the Mingo. Natty is the more successful in combating the "wicked" Indians because of his training by the Delaware, which affords him both woodland survival skills and knowledge of the Indians social and military habits – in other words, being raised by Indians provides him with "intelligence" about the enemy, as well as "special forces" training. Numerous historians emphasize that the most successful Indian fighters are those who know the Indian best and who themselves incorporate a savage element. This fact is epitomized in the Frontier Myth's hunter-hero character. "It was James Fenimore Cooper's recognition and exploitation of this figure that made his novels the seminal fictions of American literary history."[3]

But for all his respect and empathy for Indian ways, and his adaptation to woodlore and Indian philosophy, Natty Bumppo remains clearly aware of his Occidental roots, and convinced that, as far as his own soul is concerned, Christianity is the "fitting" religion for him, even if the Manitou is best suited for the Indian. In death Natty confirms this identity, rejecting Indian funeral customs. "Pawnee, I die as I have lived, a Christian man," he tells his adopted son Hard-Heart in *Pioneers*. "As I came into life, so will I leave it. Horses and arms are not needed to stand in the Presence of the Great Spirit of my people!

He knows my colour, and according to my gifts will he judge my deeds."[380-381] He chooses to rest in the Pawnee camp, i.e. to take his final root in the land he has explored and helped open; but he requests a white man's tombstone be erected on his grave, as he passes away, facing eastward, toward his beloved forests.

Likewise, while he seeks coexistence with the natives, he expresses doubt that their adaptation to white ways is sensible. Rather, each should live according to his nature and his gifts, borrowing what is practical but not abandoning self-esteem and identity. Simultaneously, he distances himself, and thereby the white American, almost as much from European superficial habits as he does the Indian. In *Deerslayer*, Chingachgook tries on a gaudy scarlet and gold-thread jacket, "not military but... part of the attire of a civilian of condition at a period when social rank was rigidly respected in dress." Natty insists:

Off with it...Such garments as little become you as they would become me. Your gifts are for paint...and mine are for doublets of skins, tough leggings, and sarvicable moccasins. I say moccasins...for though white, living as I do in the woods, it's necessary to take some of the practyces of the woods..."[201]

Chingachgook realizes the truth of these words in his last hours of life. *Pioneers* shows the once proud warrior as a degenerate relic who has lost his pride with his identity, dressing half-white, half Indian, hanging his hair over his face in shame.[79-82] On his deathbed "John Mohegan" reverts to the "Great Serpent," and once again sees his path clearly.[401]

Rejection of European Sovereignty

A major role of Leatherstocking, the man between two world's, is to act as mediator between the two, whereby he effectively translates Indian ways to the white man's benefit more often than the reverse. The ignorance of the Colonials and white Americans about their native predecessors is apparent throughout the cycle. While Bumppo frequently advises others in woodcraft, his more important role is as conduit of understanding Indian philosophy and as advocate of coexistence and mutual respect. His lecturing of Minister Grant, who displays ignorance and disdain for the native religion, is a case in point.

Leatherstocking can survive in the wilderness because he is flexible, open to new and different ways, adapting to his surroundings, both topographical and social. Europeans and Easterners who reject advice and stubbornly insist on the superiority of their own entrenched ways are doomed to perish. The fate of Corporal McNab, who dies because he will not abandon Continental drill when fighting Indians [*Pathfinder*, 310-311], symbolizes this, as does Heyward's insistence on leading the Munro party onto a "narrow and blind" path in territory he does not know, trusting in a guide whose deceitfulness should be obvious.[*Mohicans*, 2] Simultaneously these portrayals can be seen as a warning to America not to fall back into European ways of thinking or into a new orthodoxy, lest this lead the nation onto the wrong path. Thus the settlement of Templeton threatens Natty's self-worth and the identity he has carved out for himself. His values are not found in the settlement, just as America's values are not found in "settled" Europe. To preserve his soul, Natty must return to the woods, just as the United

States must turn from efforts to emulate European conventions, and return to their own true values. Interesting is the fact that Leatherstocking can adapt to Indian ways, but has problems fitting into white society – this symbolizes American rejection of European claims on the new nation's heart. Natty Bumppo's sobriquet "Pathfinder" openly plays on this role of Natty as his nation's guide.

New Names, New Beginnings

Leatherstocking undergoes numerous name changes during his life – parallel to the American people, who themselves underwent numerous identities: colonists, Puritans, cavalier planters, farmers, trappers, fortune-hunters, refugees, slave-holders, loyalists, rebels, Hamiltonian Federalists, Jeffersonian democrats, Jacksonian populists – to name just a few. Bumppo could stand for the character's lack of obvious roots, his springing from the forest like a bump on a log. Nathaniel means The Given of God, of whom Jesus said he is the prophet in whom there "is no deceit."[4] The Delaware reinforce this image by calling young Natty "Straight-Tongue" because of his honesty and forthrightness – values in accord with the drafters of the Declaration of Independence. Hawkeye could confirm not just good vision and eyesight, but "vision" and "insight" in a larger sense, as indicated by Iroquois chief Rivenoak in *Deerslayer*: "Hawkeye is right, his sight is so strong that he can see truth in a dark night..."[288]

The long list of names Natty relates in *Deerslayer* reveal the parallel evolution of a man and a nation; his seeking an "adult" name indicates an open future, not pre-ordained or selected — just as the young nation had many options, for better or worse. Everything and anything seems possible for him. In *Deerslayer*, young Leatherstocking is at his most American, his most Adamic, facing the most options while lacking experience to help him evaluate these – like the young Republic, unused to self-government, largely experimental in nature, had to rely on its selected values and its best judgement, especially of right and wrong.

Natty is aware that he is still forming, still developing: his vision is "improving, I will aknowledge; but 'tis only a child's eye, compared to some I know...Tamenund lets nothing escape his look...I'm improving, but far from being perfect, as yet."[25] The allusion to his improving ability to "see" through darkness and camouflage, in context with the reference to Tamenund, the Delaware sage and "seer," must be taken as deeper than simply meaning the young man's eyesight. Natty, who in the course of this novel acquires the appellation Hawkeye, is developing his ability to discern political and moral right and wrong, and to recognize his own true nature, just as in the 1740s (when *Deerslayer* plays) the colonies were beginning to grasp their development of interests and characteristics autonomous from England. Leatherstocking alludes to this formative status and the drifting apart from Britain again when Hetty Hutter asks his name:

That's a question more easily asked than it is answered, young woman, seeing that I'm so young and yet have born more names than some of the greatest chiefs in all America.

But you've got a name – you don't throw away one name before you come honestly by another?

I hope not, gal – I hope not. My names have come nat'rally and

CHAPTER 3

I suppose the one I bear now will be of no great lasting, since the Delawares seldom settle on a man's ra'al title until such time as he has an opportunity of showing his true natur', in the council or on the warpath.[58]

America's true identity must await the War of Independence.

Natty learns many important things about himself before the book closes. Most importantly, he learns the status and depth of his integrity. His soul and his name are "one accountable for the other," and a word given, even under duress, is a commitment not only to man (white or Indian equally), but also to God.[391] A vital piece of self-recognition comes with his statement about the Indians being mistaken if they "hold up avarice afore me on one side, and fear on t'other, and think honesty will give way atween 'em both."[312] "Conscience...is king with me, and I try never to dispute his orders."[402-403] But even much earlier he is in philosophical possession of this point, as he resists Harry's teasing about Deerslayer being a boy's name, and Natty needing to kill a man in order to prove his own manhood: "That man is the most of a man, who acts nearest the right," Natty retorts with the calm of the just.[36]

As the Pathfinder, a more mature Natty finds the proper road for himself, namely the road of self-reliance, of autonomy, refraining from entangling alliances no matter how appealing the alternative might be. "To thine own self be true" should be the foremost motto of a state, as of a man, which prides itself in adherence to principles and liberty.

Leatherstocking represents the American "new beginning," the "clean slate" on which the young nation aspired to avoid the mistakes of the past. With Leatherstocking, Cooper created a human metaphor of the United States as a character emerging spontaneously from the Earth; still growing, still searching for the ultimate form, but with high ideals and intentions, a country born consciously of its own efforts. Born of the European seed planted in the wilderness womb, the young nation bears attributes of both parents, but takes full responsibility for its own success and failures, rejecting obligation and favor arising from the past. Wayne Franklin's description of Cooper's protagonist depicts a metaphor of the young nation:

Natty Bumppo a… self-created and self-reliant [hero] who owed nothing to position; in the presence of a world where position seemed over-important, [Cooper] slowly built on the instinctual base that had sustained [this 'American'] an increasingly conscious ideology.[5]

And as the young United States was scorned by the old nations of Europe (except for Revolutionary France), Leatherstocking is considered a renegade, a primitive, or simply a "loser" by "civilized" society.[6]

Another aspect of America's "outsider" status as embodied in Leatherstocking is the fact that Natty Bumppo is an orphan, just as the Revolution "killed" the ties to the European parent. He is raised in the woods by the Delaware, but does not identify himself as one of them, either. He muses on the "gifts" he has inherited from his parents, e.g. that all Bumppos must have been good shots since he is such a marksman, but he makes little effort to really trace his roots. He is a man without roots, and, as he says of himself [*Mohicans*, 83], "without a cross" to bear, i.e. he is unburdened by the past because he has none. Like the new nation born of new (or revived) concepts, he recognizes no inheritance of guilt or responsibility for wrongs and failings of his ancestors, but looks to the present and the future. This freedom from roots, ties and shackles to the past enables him to roam at will or wherever fate takes him – like America, which has severed its ties to parent Europe in order to make its own way in the world at will. Turner identifies the constant American move westward as "an escape from the bondage of the past; and freshness, and confidence, and scorn of old society."[7] Leatherstocking therefore is, as R.W.B. Lewis terms the central figure of American literature, the "American Adam."[8] The Garden of Eden is his, and it is his own responsibility to husband it prudently, and avoid the Temptations of both savagery and decadent civilization.

The mature Leatherstocking has overcome the longing for human or social approbation. In *Pioneers*, he says:

When I first came into the woods to live, I used to have weak spells when I felt lonesome: and then I would go into the Catskills, and spend a few days on that hill to look at the ways of man; but it's now many a year since I felt any such longings...[280]

This again is an admonition to America to cut off any residual emotional longing for Europe, or for acceptance or approval by Europe, whether on a political or on a cultural level. America, like Natty, can be and should be autonomous. A few days study of European ways should suffice to convince Americans that they do not really aspire to association or "acceptance" in this way. Or as he tells Ishmael in *Prairie*: "I see little difference in nations."[76] In other words, the United States does not acknowledge any inherent superiority by one nation over others, and asserts its natural rights as equal among the older states. America has overcome the stage of political nonentity it carried as a colony, embodied in young Deerslayer's confession: "because I'm not born a redskin, [I] have no right to sit in their councillings, and am much too humble to be called on for opinions from the great of my own color."[58]

No Entangling Alliances

Leatherstocking's apparent virginity can be seen as a metaphor of American political morality (or at least the belief in and yearning for it). The American protagonist's marriage would force him to adapt to "foreign" (i.e. his wife's) influences and values. Leatherstocking, as the "American Adam," is wiser than his Biblical forefather, and strives to avoid the Fall. The isolated America withstands external temptation. Deerslayer's decision to remain free of the entangling and enticing arms of Judith Hutter symbolizes the American path of self-determination, free from the luxurious, decadent aspects of Europe embodied by her. The same holds for his decision in *Pathfinder* to rescind his wedding plans. Marriage to Mabel Dunham would have required settling down, abandoning his philosophy of being one with Nature, taking only what he needs for the moment, neither appropriating nor changing what he found. It would have required giving up his ideals and being morally compromised. Even the courting brings Natty temporarily down, costing him self-respect, undermining his fieldcraft, distracting from his duties as scout, filling him with self-doubts and dread (he dreams of firing at a deer, and missing).[407] Natty's vigor suffers through idleness and vanity, until he loses his betrothed to Jasper just in time. His worldview had been distorted, but in the end he relinquishes his illusions and so escapes death and impotence – just as the United States finally escaped national or cultural death by overcoming the clinging influences of England.

The American independence of mind is primarily a question of self-confidence, of faith in the correctness of the chosen path. Here, again, Leatherstocking's stoic surety in the legitimacy of his decisions frees him from anxious misgivings and indecision. This is the route Cooper would see for America, given the nation's fidelity to its principles. America, like Leatherstocking, need not vie for foreign approval. "[Leatherstocking] judges himself not on the social standard of competition with [other men], but on the artist's standard of perfection."[9] He requires no third-party applause to know he is acting properly. He measures success with the difficulty of the task at hand and in terms of comparison with himself, not with others, a concept which would be irrelevant for him. He is good, and he knows it. Anan. Enough.

This does not mean that Natty rejects his European inheritance. On the contrary – he retains that which is good, and frequently speaks proudly of his "white gifts." Cooper explained this aspect of the Leatherstocking character in 1850:

The idea of delineating a character that possessed little of civilization but its highest principles as they are exhibited in the uneducated and all of the savage life that is not incompatible with these great rules of conduct, is perhaps natural to the situation in which Natty was placed. He is too proud of his origin to sink into the condition of the wild Indian, and too much a man of the woods not to imbibe as much as was at all desirable, from his friends and companions. In a moral point of view, it was the intention to illustrate the effect of seeds scattered by the wayside. To use his own language, his 'gifts' were 'white gifts,' and he was not disposed to bring on them discredit. On the other hand, removed from nearly all the temptations of civilized life, placed in the best associations of that which is deemed savage, and favorably disposed by nature to improve such advantages,, it appeared to the writer that his hero was a fit subject to represent the better qualities of both conditions without pushing either to extremes.[10]

Nature and Order

This again is a logical aspect of the American character. The Declaration of Independence had its roots in the classical education of its authors, who liberally borrowed from Greek, Roman, and Old Testament principles. America's Revolution was thus not a repudiation of European values, but a return to the purest principles underlying Western civilization, which had become corrupted over the preceding fifteen-odd centuries. Sons of the Enlightenment, the Founding Fathers recognized that the roots of classical civilization were not far removed from the Laws of Nature, if the latter were defined as a divine order from which Europe, in the course of civilization, had departed.[11] The synthesis of the finest aspects of Western society and Natural Law to a new, higher order seemed only logical. This is what Leatherstocking, Adamic but not void, represents. The justification of Natty's disaffection with civilization is presented, for example, through the behavior displayed by Harry and Hutter in *Deerslayer*: Natty kills out of necessity, and refuses to scalp; the Indians (even the enemies) kill because they are at war, and scalp because it is part of their culture; Hutter and Harry, however, kill and scalp women and children for "rational" purposes, namely the bounty which the "civilized" British government has put up for such scalps, no questions asked.[41-42] Cooper need explicitly say no more to delineate who has departed most from natural morality – the "savage" or the herald of "civilization."

The Prairie presents another example of Natty's inherent belief in the superior aspects of Natural Law, which are practiced by the Indian. His rhetorical allusion to the Fifth Commandment (p. 82) presumes the validity of paternal-filial loyalty, and in extension, the basic social responsibilities within family and society – responsibilities ignored through corruption, perversion, greed, as epitomized by the "authorities" in *Pioneers* or by the scalpers bounties in *Deerslayer*. Ishmael Bush's intimidation of his sons, which after the confrontation with Asa becomes apparent as the source for their "voiceless conformity," is another example of the violation of the paternal-filial bond of mutual obligation – and a warning not to allow "authority" to usurp the basic freedom of thought and speech inherent in the American Dream and in the Constitution. Ishmael, the rebel against outside authority, has displayed himself as a tyrant in his own right – Leatherstocking serves to illuminate this point, to awaken the victims of this rebellious oppressor, to their fate and to their rights, and to warn the "authority" that his heavy hand will inspire revolt in his own sons, just as the hand of Ishmael's father inspired Ishmael's own escape. Natty in contrast sets a good example in *Pathfinder* by releasing Mabel Dunham from the obligation of her domineering father's wish that she marry the Leatherstocking; the woodsman who cherishes his own freedom and human dignity realizes that coercion, whether physical, legal, or moral, is not in accordance with the natural justice he believes in.[409 ff.]

Mirror of American History and Politics

The *Leatherstocking Tales* parallel major phases of political and socio-economic development of America, up to and including Cooper's lifetime. Warren Motley agrees with Edwin Fussell and Henry Nash that:

The frontier was the expressive emblem of dialectical tensions between the Old World and the New, past and future, order and liberty...surrounding the invention of a new culture. Novels in which the frontier provides scenario and setting as well as metaphor let writers test, in an almost experimental way, the cohesive or divisive effects of specific social values from one generation to the next.[12]

Westward Expansion

British colonial policy had restricted expansion of settlement.[13] This was justified by treaties with Indian nations, and with the diplomatic implications of extending British settlement areas to or beyond implied or declared borders of French dominion. A major reason was London's fear of losing control over settlers who moved outside of the reach of colonial authorities, perhaps even to pact with foreign powers or assert independence. Benjamin Franklin's consistent argument that the colonies' population doubled every twenty-five years, requiring eventual expansion to the Mississippi and acquisition of Canada for the Crown, raised eyebrows and tempers in London. An anti-expansionist pamphleteer wrote in 1761:

America as she rises to maturity, may endanger our trade and liberty both. It must be absurd to say or think, that when America exceeds us in numbers of people, that she will nevertheless continue dependent...Let no man flatter himself with these empty phantoms, or fancy that he can alter the nature and passions of men, or make them more fond of dependencey in a collective body, than individuals are: it must appear equally absurd to imagine, that North America as she advances in agriculture, and encreases in numbers of people, will not also encrease in industry, arts, trades, manufactures and sciences...[14]

The decades following national independence witnessed a major thrust westward. The Trans-Allegheny Frontier, which marked the edge of settlement from the opening of the Northwest Territories by the Ordinance of 1787 until around 1800, was followed by the Mississippi Valley Frontier opened after the Louisiana Purchase. This region sufficed to absorb most settler-emigration for the following two decades, leaving further regions to trappers and the like. These decades also witnessed considerable conflict between landholders and speculators, especially large land companies, and individual farmers who often had little understanding or patience regarding legalities such as land title. Popular demand for free and equal access to public lands, and for "squatters' rights," marked this era. The 1830s and 1840s subsequently saw wholesale disposition of western land as a reaction to these tensions. Cooper recognized the dangers and fallacy of uncontrolled "taming" of natural resources which could never be restored after the fact, and presented his concerns with such "wasty" policies through Leatherstocking.[15]

Closely linked is Natty's identification with Nature itself. Leatherstocking's mythic aura is enhanced by the way Cooper portrays him as an organic part of the forest, from which he emerges at the beginning of several books, and into which he blends again at the end. The location of the young to middle-aged, dynamic Leatherstocking in the forests, and the old Natty in the clearing and on the prairie, also associates the ancient forest with the concept of youth, of life – the unspoiled eastern section of America in which the young colonies and young nation had so many opportunities to choose their future course. Natty's reverence for the forest as if it were an entity is evident from the brotherly way he speaks of it. "I've no land to clear; and Heaven knows I would rather set out six trees afore I would cut one down," he says in *Pioneers* [319].

But the question of natural preservation can also be seen as retaining political undertones. If the strong (the Settlers) are allowed to exploit the erstwhile defenseless Nature just to satisfy their whims, how can these same settlers recognize their own exploitation by those more powerful, and how could they justify protesting against it? The Pigeon shoot in *Pioneers* [231 ff.], killing off thousands of the "feathered tribe" [with a cannon!] for sport, not for need, bears strong symbolic reference to the genocide against the Indian; the fishing scene [246 ff.] refers to the netted fish as "alarmed victims" struggling "in fruitless efforts for freedom" – the fate of the American citizen if he allows despotic rule to creep into power?

By the People, For the People

Inherent also in the political and social process of America, from Revolutionary times until today, is the dichotomy between the principles of government and self-determination, between "man's law" and "God's law" or "natural law." Natty's soliloquy about laws sometimes being a necessary evil, especially to protect the weak, still emphasizes his classification of man's laws, and their instruments of enforcement, as inherently negative. His struggle with Richard Jones, the Sheriff in *Pioneers*, and the hapless way Judge Temple feels compelled to do wrong, against his own wishes, in the name of the law, underscores this theme. In *Pioneers* Natty voices disillusionment with the new political system created in America: "...Times be altering in these mountains from what they was thirty years ago, or for that matter, ten years. But might makes right, and the law be stronger than an old man, whether he is one that has much larning, or only one like me..."[129] He perceives abuse of the legal system to the advantage of a new socio-economic elite. "You may make your laws, Judge, but...I think one old law is worth two new ones...Your titles and your farms are all new together, but laws should be equal, and not more for one than another."[153][16]

He leaves no doubt as to his priorities: "When the colony's laws, or even the King's laws, run ag'in the laws of God, they got to be onlawful, and ought not to be obeyed," young Natty firmly states in *Deerslayer*.[42] Even feeling his own strength, and capacity to fend for himself, waning, he refers in *Pioneers* to the law as a necessary evil to protect the weak and dependent.[27]

A related topic is Natty's self-sufficiency, contrasted with the paternalistic approach of Judge Temple. Both remember the virgin land they entered brief decades earlier, but differ in the appropriate future policy; Natty trusts in Providence, which he believes benevolent,[17] and wants to leave Nature as it is, while the Judge wishes to cultivate and develop the land to provide for the populace. Natty believes that every true man fends for himself; the Judge wishes to provide for others, which in Natty's view results in the loss of the beneficiaries' freedom and self-esteem.

This suspicion of civil authority is only natural in a nation which bases its existence on the rejection of and rebellion against a system which, in its fundamentals, had been accepted as proper for millennia. Early American government, in particular, had to find a way to re-introduce the concept of loyalty to the state, of subordination of the individual to a greater secular entity, while retaining the validity of the Revolution which had created the new nation. Cooper rightly takes up the concept as one of the great American questions. Motley places Cooper not only with the great philosophical *romanciers* of America, but also with great political thinkers and activists such as Jackson and Lincoln, because of the ambivalence toward authority displayed through the *Leatherstocking Tales*, marked by patriarchs on one hand, and Natty's refusal to submit to outside authority and his successive breaks with society on the other.[18]

New Aristocracy?

Related to this question of legal and government authority is the concept of class. Within white society, Cooper portrays three major groups: the genteel classes representative of his own background – educated landowners, military leaders, and holders of public office; "good" whites of lower class, yeoman farmers who work honestly, "know their place," and defer to their social betters; and "primitive" whites (squatters, scalpers, and other semi-criminal elements) who assume the negative aspects of Indian behavior without displaying the positive elements of Indian nature. Outside these greater groupings stands Natty Bumppo as a collective conscious. Natty's consistent reference to the abuse of nature by the encroaching settlers can also be seen as a reference to the ignoring of the need for a "natural order" within society, based not on the letter of man-made laws, so open to abuse at the hands of the weak (Judge

Temple) or the vicious (Sheriff Richard Jones and Assistant Justice Hiram Doolittle), but on the principle of natural leaders, well-intentioned, without pretense, who accept guidance from the wise, informed persona represented by the unpretentious scout. In other words, natural leaders, of the George Washington ilk, should retain power, and be guided by the noble traditions and thoughts of the Declaration of Independence, the natural yet classical American Spirit represented by Leatherstocking.

This aspect of Leatherstocking as guiding spirit for the new nation is obvious in the appearance of three generations of Heywards and Middletons in various books of the series. Major Duncan Heyward, the well-intentioned but naive British officer who displays ignorance and disorientation about the Wilderness in *Mohicans* is revealed in *Pioneers* as having joined the Patriots in the War of Independence:

He was then an Officer of the King; but when the war took place between the Crown and her Colonies, my grandfather did not forget his birthplace, but threw off the empty allegiance of names and was true to his proper country; he fought on the side of Liberty.[112]

Duncan Uncas Middleton proudly relates this to Natty, who replies, in congruence with Deerslayer's address to Hetty Hutter: "There was reason in it; and what is better, there was Natur."[112] The education Duncan Heyward received from Natty opened up his eyes to the true nature of America, and the hollowness of the remaining bonds to Britain. The experience of *Mohicans*, under Leatherstocking's influence, awakened Heyward to his American identity.

In *Pioneers*, Leatherstocking acts to mend the rift between loyalist and rebel which marred the domestic cohesion of the young United States. By guiding Oliver Effingham to reconciliation with Judge Temple, and marriage with Temple's daughter,

Natty sets the path for mending wounds and building national identity.

The Pioneers simultaneously addresses several of the domestic conflicts inherent in early United States society (and which have repeated themselves over the course of American history). Underlying the entire novel is the theme of political legitimacy and economic domination, represented by control over land.

Judge Temple, despite his Whig identity, represents the failings of the European, traditional system: he secures appointments for incompetent or dishonest officials, including his own cousin, Sheriff Jones; hypocritically registers his slave in his cousin's name in order to overcome the Quaker ban on slave-ownership; places the letter of the law over justice, even imposing a harsher sentence on Natty than he would have to. A self-made man from simple background, Marmaduke Temple assumes airs of aristocracy – it is no coincidence that his first name is frequently reduced to "Duke." Woodcutters doff their caps as his sleigh passes, and the village women and children "throng to the windows to witness the arrival of their landlord and his daughter."[53-55] Even accepting his basic good intentions, Temple is rife for displacement because he is not competent to protect the people of Templeton from the connivance of Jones and Co.

Natty's burning of his own hut, rather than allowing Assistant Justice Hiram Doolittle to force entry after swindling a search warrant out of Judge Temple, signals his dissolution of all ties with the community, since he thus rids himself of the only property he could not carry.[340-341] This act contains a significant development:

The fire marks the end of an era in which a man could peacefully enjoy his own property; it signals the failure of the government.

CHAPTER 3

For the law, strong enough to punish Natty for killing a deer out of season, is inadequate to justice or to the essential function of government.[19]

Hiram's wheedling of the search warrant, his needless invasion of Natty's cabin, his provoking the old man into pushing him so Natty might be arrested and charged with resisting the law – all these smack harshly of the violation of colonial homes which provided a rallying point for the Declaration of Independence. Abuse of the system by those in power or by those able to manipulate officeholders bode ill for the basic premise of the nation.

[1] See William Gilmore Simm's preface to The Yemassee, Nathaniel Hawthorne's preface to The House of the Seven Gables, and Owen Wister's introduction to The Virginian for the shared opinion that the Romance must present "the truth of the heart" (Hawthorne) even if it swerves from the factual depiction of historical events. Summarized in Folsom, pp. 19. ff.

[2] House,, p. 6, and Ch. 1 passim; also see Folsom, pp. 44 ff., for elaboration on this concept. Also Franklin, p.34, on Natty Bumppo as an "ideological" character.

[3] Slotkin, p. 80

[4] Cited in House, p. 283.

[5] Franklin, p. 34. See also Lawrence, pp. 59-60, on the concept of rebirth as essential to the American Myth.

[6] [1]. See Lewis, pp. 85 ff., on the "outsider" as the true American hero; But see Slotkin, pp. 129 ff., for discussion of equally negative portrayal of woodsmen as renegades and sociopaths in mid-19th-century American writing, e.g. R.M. Bird's *Nick of the Woods* (1837) and James Hall's *Indian Hater* (1835).

These writers also consistently portrayed native Americans as savages without redeeming characteristics.

[7] F.J. Turner, "Significance," quoted in Barker, p. 11.

[8] Lewis, passim, but here p. 89

[9] House, p. 266.

[10] Cooper, Preface to the Leatherstocking Tales, 1850; quoted in Meserole, pp. 807-810.

[11] The concept of a Natural Divine Order was not new. One earlier example is Charlemagne's experiment of raising children in total silence, expecting them to automatically speak Hebrew, then considered the language of Creation and thus the "natural" language of mankind.

[12] Motley, p. 5.

[13] The Royal Writ of 1763 was the last such regulation limiting westward expansion of American settlements, and exacerbated tensions between London and the assertive colonies.

[14] "Reasons for Keeping Guadaloupe at a Peace, preferable to Canada, Explained in Five Letters from a Gentleman in Guadaloupe, to His Friend in London," cited in Draper, pp. 16-18.

[15] For discussion of the phases of expansion, see Folsom, passim; Franklin, pp. 212 ff.; Leisy, pp. 114-117; Taylor, Town, Introduction. Also Slotkin, passim, for discussion of the class-dominated struggle over land as a major element of 19th-Century American politics, and its place in the American Myth and corresponding literature.

[16] A different edition of *Pioneers* has Natty say, even more critically, "might often makes right here, as well as in the old country, for what I can see."

[17] See, for example, his conversation with Heyward in the ruins of Fort William Henry, Mohicans, pp. 228-29.

CHAPTER 3

[18] Motley, pp. 10, 23. Also see House, p. 299
[19] House, pp. 270-71.

Chapter 4

VISION OF A NEW ORDER

Synthesis and Self-Determination

Crevecour's question "what is an American?" lies at the heart of American literature, i.e. that literature which is particular to this country, which could have been written nowhere else, regardless of any universal themes it might include. Folsom points out that this question is frequently reformulated into "What should an American be?" Cooper addresses primarily the latter as he develops Leatherstocking as a New Man, a synthesis of ancient and modern, savage and civilized, philosopher and practician, pacifist and warrior – in Fussel's words, "America as it should be." Cooper saw the primary obligation of America in creating this "New Man," in defining his integrity and purpose and values – only when this was resolved would it make sense to work on the superficial trappings of society. Balzac termed Natty "a magnificent hermaphrodite, born between the savage and the civilized states of man."[1]

Natty and his Indian friends converse and live as equals. Cooper realizes that the Indian as free entity is doomed from the beginning of European expansion in the New World. At best, he will be assimilated into a new, harmonious relationship in a new social order, dominated by white values tempered by Native aspects. At worst, he will be destroyed. Leatherstocking, as agent of change against his own will, contributes to this development. If he succeeds as mediator, he will initiate the native's assimilation, and loss of independent identity; if he fails as mediator, his role as trailblazer for civilization will result in the military victory over the native. His friendship with Chingachgook cannot change this inevitable course of events. Cooper subtly points out how Natty, as explorer and forerunner of the settlers and military, initiates this fall of the native from the very beginning, by giving young Natty the sobriquet "Deerslayer." Natty the scout, the white woodsman bearing his trusty rifle "Killdeer," thus is given primary blame for the death of the last of the Mohicans. By opening up the wilderness, he makes inevitable the death of Uncas, "le cerf agile" – "the nimble stag." Leatherstocking is, as *Pioneers* concludes, "the foremost in that band of pioneers who are opening the way for the march of the nation across the continent."[436]

Yet the role of the white hunter as mediator between his own people and the natives is essential for the self-respect of the white conscious, for America's acceptance of its own legitimacy in conquering the continent. Despite the white dispossession of the natives, "the mediation of Leatherstocking suggests that this process involves - below the violence - a passing on of legitimate authority from the elder race to the younger."[2] Natty's view of himself in *Mohicans* as a second father for Uncas, whose name is a generic denomination for "Chief," and his later adoption of Hard-Heart in *Prairie*, indicate a symbolic attempt to assimilate the Indian under a benevolent and understanding wing before the opportunity would be lost forever in a campaign of extermination or subjugation.

And Leatherstocking himself, this most perfect of white men, who absorbs the best of the Native while rejecting the bad of both races, becomes the torch, the vessel of this new legitimate authority and all it entails – he is the ideal new man, the American. D.H. Lawrence recognizes Cooper's vision of the ideal new nation to come, someday:

The white man's spirit can never become as the red man's spirit. It doesn't want to. But it can cease to be the opposite and the negative of the red man's spirit. It can open out a new great area of consciousness, in which there is room for the red spirit too.[3]

As mediator between European and primitive societies and ways, Leatherstocking tries to show the way to a new, superior order which must arise from synthesis of the two, since destruction of the one by the other will only lead to repetition of past mistakes in previous societies; America owes itself and its Revolution the effort of creating a new society, better than the one the early pioneers and European emigrants left, or the one they found in the New World. Without this goal, the Revolution will have been for naught, nothing but a rising led by merchants and landowners for the sake of their own power and benefits.

This is the reason for Cooper's use of historical setting and sequences to portray America and the factors of historical determination – how the nation became what it is, what it could be, and how it could realize its full potential. He also wishes to show how America must pick and choose from its various heritages, to become, as Leatherstocking, a nation with all the best traits of its ancestors and brothers, but none of the worst. This opportunity to pick and choose, to consciously shape oneself, is the essence of the American Dream, on a national and individual scale.

Cooper describes a vision of a new order, for order there must be, even if it goes against the anarchistic streak of woodsmen and squatters. But the American order should be a meritocracy determined to work toward the common good, not the good of particular classes, regions, or (despite the actual course of events) racial and ethnic groups. This American vision aimed for empowerment of "natural rulers," so called "military aristocrats" as depicted through Oliver Effingham (*Pioneers*), Captain Middleton (*Prairie*), and Duncan Heyward (*Mohicans*). These enlightened, progressive individuals would stand above the primitive conditions inherent in the Frontier, but would reject the self-serving decadence of European hereditary aristocracy. "The white Frontiersman (Leatherstocking) would act as mediator, synthesizing (and fading away) with the primitive, but breaking trail [for progress]."[4] Natty explains this concept to the "aristocratic" young Heyward in *Mohicans* [66-67], telling how Indian names reflect an individual's expertise, and how the Indians and he can thus be considered an aristocracy of talent. The same is related in *Deerslayer* regarding the selection of chiefs, not through heredity, but on grounds of merit.[475] In addition to honoring achievement, this system forced the individual to recognize his strengths and weaknesses, and to strive for excellence with honor in order to live up to the granted name and reputation. In *Prairie* he proclaims calmly: "various have been the names by which I have gone through life...I humbly trust I shall be able to answer to any of mine in a loud and manly voice."[171] But simultaneously, the Indian concept of honor is shown to be less superficial than the European: "Duncan [Heyward] has accepted society's standards of honorable conduct and is consequently concerned about how his actions appear to others; for Natty, the importance of honor is psychological and personal rather than social."[5] He expresses this in *Mohicans* with "it is better for a man to die at peace with himself than to live haunted by an evil conscience."[92] Cooper thus reveals more substance in the natural, more show in the civilized [European] approach to honor.

That the new American nation must proudly build on the legacies of two cultures, European and Indian, to form a third, superior order, is presented in the proud manner in which the young natural leaders speak of their association with the Indians. Oliver Effingham boasts of being the descendant of a great Delaware chief, and of being of Delaware blood, although he is fully white; his father was accepted into the Delaware nation, and young Oliver simply adopts his Indian name.[*Pioneers*, 135, 383-385] Three of Major Duncan Hayward's descendants bear the middle-name Uncas.[*Prairie*, 112] Natty's tutorship has contributed largely to this positive attitude and vision of a just and wise nation. He has done all he can do on Earth, and must pass the torch to his disciples. However he was called, this perfect man is able to fulfill his wish and answer his Maker "with a voice that might be heard in every part of that numerous assembly...'Here!'"[385]

Buckskin Prophet

Cooper conceived Leatherstocking as an allegorical figure, metaphysical in his stoic detachment, his status above the baser instincts. Natty is a participant in America's development, as he must be to serve the readers as a guiding thread through the great American story; yet he is also an observer, providing philosophical insight through his commentaries, simple in form but deep in substance.

Cooper makes no secret of this special nature. In the Preface to the *Tales*, written in 1850, well after the novels, he tells how Bumppo was conceived as a creation possessing the "better qualities" of both the white and red races, but no negative traits of either. Folsom notes Natty remains:

unalloyed with the gift to do evil which is a necessary result of the imperfect nature of our common humanity; and Cooper removes him from society, placing him between red men and white, so that Natty' comments may be upon the failures of both... Cooper must remove Natty as far as possible from direct involvement in the world about him in order that he may more objectively comment upon it; for his perspective is the unbiased and clear perspective of history upon the confused world of event.[6]

The metaphysical elements of Leatherstocking are underscored by his propensity to appear out of the green when needed, only to fade back into nature like a shadow when his mission is accomplished – when the helpless are safe, the wrongs righted, the nature of justice and injustice explained, even if not resolved – a guardian angel or the good spirit of the land. This picture is most graphically developed in the opening of the *Prairie*, where Natty emerges as an awesome figure magnified by the light, outlined against the sky, mysterious until the end of the chapter. Leatherstocking is the Spirit of '76 incarnate, come to Earth to guide by his example and philosophy, but also to experience firsthand the realities and difficulties of the path he represents.

On a more earthly level, young Natty portrays the national, independent-minded spirit of the colonies in the years before Revolution. He cooperates with the British authorities, but operates autonomously from them. In *Deerslayer* he (like Hurry Harry) deliberately misleads the authorities concerning the real lay of the land beyond that surveyed by the government, in an attempt to keep the land free from official control. During wartime, he guides British forces, but the distance which has already arisen between the American and the Briton is evident in the disdain Leatherstocking displays for the arrogant and foolhardy operations and manners of the European soldiers. Aligned with American nature and assimilated into Native ways, Leatherstocking represents an America which has developed into a third party, separate from both the British and the French, merely waiting to realize and articulate this separateness.

Leatherstocking represents the nucleus of the new society – not necessarily as it was or would be, but as it should be, as it had the potential to become. The symbolic friendship among equals between Natty and Chingachgook is the dream of the union of positive ideals into a new society, as the two men absorb from one-another. The image of Chingachgook as "the Great Serpent" paints him as Natty's mirror-image. A snake grows a new skin beneath the old, which it sheds when it is ready. As Natty bears occidental traits and values beneath the wilderness buckskin dress he acquired from the Delaware, so Chingachgook accepts white aspects beneath his skin. In *Pioneers*, the Indian has shed his original skin for "white" clothes, Christian religion, and an English name. In the end, he reverts to his true basic values, repudiating what was not natural for him. But he lives on in his brother Natty, to whom he has bequeathed his knowledge and his spirit. Within Natty, the two souls blend to form "the new nucleus of a new society, the clue to a new world order. It asks for a great and cruel sloughing first of all. Then it finds a great release into a new world, a new moral, a new landscape."[7] America as it could be, as it should be – the best of both worlds.

[1] Cited by Grossman, p. 147. Also see House, Ch. 1
  [2] Slotkin, p. 129
  [3] Lewis, p. 57.
  [4] Slotkin, p. 500.
  [5] House, p. 283.
  [6] Folsom, pp. 55 ff.
  [7] Lawrence, pp. 59-60.

Chapter 5

COOPER - THE FIRST AMERICAN NOVELIST

Alfred Tressidar Sheppard, doyen of literary history, speaks for numerous scholars when he states that "American fiction began with the historical novel."[1] Professor Richard Slotkin speaks for many scholars of early United States literature and history when he writes:[2]

It might be said of James Fenimore Cooper that if he had not existed, it would have been necessary to invent him. Few writers have deserved the name of literary pioneer, and few have had his influence on the mythological vocabulary and generic structure of their culture's literature...No American writer before Cooper made so exact use of the materials of American history, none created works that equal popularity and respectability, and none sustained so large and thematically coherent a body of work.

Cooper's view of the nature of history and of the ironies inherent in it is one of his major influences on American literature.

He escaped the specter of America's lacking castles and princes by emphasizing that historical perspective is really created by event rather than by the mere accumulation of centuries. "The passage of time was significant only insofar as it of necessity produced the passage of event. But in a land where events move rapidly, a real history is created even without the passage of a great amount of time."[3]

Certainly history of the young American nation passed in more concentrated form than elsewhere; whether on the backrooms of Boston or at the source of the Susquehanna, the compact, but therefore all the more intense events defining the emergence and forming of the new nation bore no less intrigue, danger, violence, and general human interest than Europe's, castles or no. The emergence of a self-confident American literature required the insight that history is made by people: all else constitutes props. Cooper overcame the inherent lack of confidence of American cultural leaders, and proclaimed national cultural independence proudly.

On the political level, Cooper dealt with the major issues of his time, and with a visionary eye, recognized the implications of these issues for the nation's future. His immediate and long-term popularity testify to his fiction's touching deep-seated strands of the national conscious:

At bottom, it was the compatibility of the Cooperian myth code with reality that made the fictions of the Laird of Cooperstown (and his imitators) more than an ephemeral fashion in literary taste. The persistence of Cooper is in part explained by the persistence of the concerns, conditions, and beliefs that Cooper addressed."[4]

Central to this concern is Leatherstocking's role as guide, as pathfinder for the reader through the forest of American history and experience. "Indeed, Cooper's most important contribution to later Western story is that he manages to create a way of looking at the events of American history which can make some kind of philosophical sense out of them."[5]

Cooper's intent here is most openly stated on the first page of *Deerslayer*:

On the human imagination events produce the effects of time. Thus, he who has travelled far and seen much is apt to fancy that he has lived long, and the history that most abounds in important incidents soonest assumes the aspect of antiquity. In no other way can we account for the venerable air that is already gathering around American annals. When the mind reverts to the earliest days of colonial history, the period seems remote and obscure, the thousand changes that thicken long the links of recollections throwing back the origin of the nation to a day so distant as seemingly to reach the mists of time...[9]

The significance of these words is all the greater given the dual nature of *Deerslayer*; the last written novel of the cycle simultaneously displays the oldest setting and the youngest, most innocent manifestation of Leatherstocking/America, who loses his innocence (but not his purity) here. It takes America to its origins, the jumping off point where the individual character of the nation, growing from the combination of Occidental roots nurtured by savage stepparents, begins to emerge. The deliberate reference to "antiquity" and "the mists of time" places America on an equal footing with Greece and Rome, justifying the American claim to equality with the nations of Europe. Chancellor James Kent, a famed judge, toasted Cooper in 1826 before the author's trip to Europe: "The genius which has rendered our native soil classic ground, and given to our early history the enchantments of fiction."[6]

This role of Cooper as a national writer in more than one sense of the term is not coincidental. Cooper himself refers to his political intentions in contributing to development of a national, a patriotic literature. While his national fervor grew even more intense during his extended stay in Europe,[7] after the first three Leatherstocking novels were written, he earlier speaks directly of his intention to prove that American authors could treat American themes to create American novels of at least equal merit with British literature, assuming the daunting "task of making American manners and American scenes interesting to an American reader."[8] In 1820 Cooper wrote: "Books are, in a great measure, the instruments of controlling the opinions of a nation like ours. They are an engine alike powerful to save or destroy."[9] He thus came, almost by default, to stand at the fore of the nascent movement of literary nationalism which developed within the decade following victory in the War of 1812, America's second war of independence. As historian Francis Parkman wrote, Cooper became the first New World writer to engrave images on the hearts of his compatriots.[10]

The victory over Britain in 1815 secured American independence, both politically and psychologically. A wave of self-confidence and national identity of the diverse states emerged, perhaps most visibly expressed in the Monroe Doctrine pronounced in 1823. It can hardly be considered coincidence that the rise of American national literature, with the first decade of Cooper's writing, falls together with proclamation of the Monroe Doctrine – a dual "hands off" declaration by an American people become aware it can stand on its own feet, both militarily and culturally. Cooper's work fulfilled the now awakened desire, hunger, need for literary expression of their new self-awareness.[11]

Cognizant of the thirst of Americans for a national focus

deeper than the intellectual appeal of political theory, and of the significance of national icons appealing to the subconscious, "Cooper crafted a reassuring past intended to secure the republic's future stability. He understood that people sought the future based upon a collective identity derived from narratives that made sense of their past; histories shaped the trajectory of the nation's future."[12] Channing equated the task of forging a national cultural identity with the achievement of national political existence – not a task of reform, but of creation.[13]

The white society Natty faces is frequently corrupt, greedy, wasty, and/or overregulated by laws and government which mock justice. This society represents the Europe from which America broke away, but to which the young nation surreptitiously looked to for recognition, as a child hopes to win grace in the eyes of parents after leaving home. The red society contrasts not unfavorably with the white. Its is a harsh, but fair, "noble" savagery governed by Natural Law which seem more just and more direct. Leatherstocking recognizes that man's true potential lies in taking these Natural or Divine Laws and preserving them while utilizing the best which "civilization" has to offer – Natty, rooted in two worlds and simultaneously in none, has, like America, the best option of making a fresh start, keeping the best and tossing the rest from both worlds.

In later years Cooper despaired at developments in his country, even being attacked as a renegade for his attempts at constructive criticism. Writing *The Prairie*, originally planned as the final episode in Natty Bumppo's saga, the author still believed that the good spirit of America might guide the nation onto the proper path. Young Duncan Uncas Middleton, named for his grandfather Duncan Heyward and for the memory of noble Uncas, can be seen as being influenced by the memory and moral specter of Leatherstocking; although he never met Natty before the events of the novel, he was reared on stories about the scout, "a man endowed with the choicest and perhaps rarest gift of nature: that of distinguishing good from evil."[114] Obviously the young man's parents felt this way. The fact that they named their son after Uncas is a sign of hope, of a synthesized American society which might come to life in future generations. In this case, Natty's spiritual bequest would have taken fruit.

This vision of the United States as a melting pot, with liberty and justice for all, is no less valid today than 150 years ago. America is simultaneously blessed and burdened by greater ethnic and national heterogeneity than ever before. The challenge of realizing the American experiment of as nearly perfect a society as possible seems overwhelming – as overwhelming as the potential rewards of a nation which could draw upon the best the world has to offer.

Writers dream of creating the "great American Novel." Maybe it would be an exaggeration to claim that Cooper created it 160 years ago with his multi-volume *Leatherstocking Tales*. Maybe. Anan. Enough.

[1] Sheppard, p. 59
  [2] Slotkin, p. 81.
  [3] Folsom, p. 39.
  [4] Slotkin, p. 109. See also Meserole, pp. 805-806.
  [5] Folsom, p. 37.
  [6] Cited in Grossman, p. 50.
  [7] See, for example, Slotkin, pp. 82 ff; Spiller, *Critic*.
  [8] Referring to his second novel and first historical romance,

The Spy, 1821; Quoted in Taylor, p. 408.

[9] Taylor, p. 423.

[10] Cited in Lewis, p. 99. Also see House, pp. 4 ff., on Cooper's conscious determination to help his countrymen achieve "mental independence."

[11] For discussion of the ready reception afforded Cooper, and its reasons, see Taylor, 409 ff. For the overall impact of the War of 1812 on American society, see Lecky; for the War as impetus development of national cultural consciousness, see Spiller, <u>Revolution</u>, Introduction and Ch. 1. For discussion of Cooper's status as *the* first American novelist, see, inter alia, Barker, pp. 27 ff.; House, Ch. 1; Leisy, pp. 10-11; Perkins, p. 805 ff.; Sheppard, pp. 57-58; Taylor, pp. 409 ff.

[12] Taylor, "Fenimore Cooper's America," p. 27.

[13] Channing, "Reflections."

Milton Keynes UK
Ingram Content Group UK Ltd.
UKHW051357301124
451917UK00018B/181